NATIONAL
GEOGRAPHIC

T0288721

Ice

Belle Perez

Ice is frozen water.
Ice can be found in the sky,
on the land, and in the water.

snowflake

Snow is made of ice.
Snowflakes are tiny pieces of ice
that fall from the sky.

hailstones

Hail is made of ice.
Hailstones are balls of ice that fall
from the sky.

A **glacier** is made of ice.
A glacier is ice that covers a large area of land.

An **iceberg** is made of ice.
An iceberg is a large chunk of ice
that floats in the ocean.

All these things are made of ice.

snow

hail

glacier

iceberg

Trucks have **big** wheels, too.

This scooter has *little* wheels.

Skateboards have *little* wheels, too.

How are **wheels** the same?

Some wheels are **little**.

Some wheels are **big**.